CW01498185

Original title:

What's the Point? A Life's Guide to Uncertainty

Author: Rafael Sterling

ISBN HARDBACK: 978-1-80566-086-6

ISBN PAPERBACK: 978-1-80566-381-2

The Elusive Thread

Life's a game of hide and seek,
Chasing whispers, not a peak.
Stitching moments, loopy seams,
Woven chaos fills our dreams.

Grab a needle, take a chance,
Dance through life, a silly dance.
Twists and turns, a tangled net,
What's next? A toss-up, I bet.

Dreams on a Winding Road

Driving through the twists and bends,
Life's GPS just pretends.
Maps are scribbles, coffee spills,
Who needs direction when it thrills?

Potholes bounce the laughter loud,
Detours make the strangest crowd.
Lost my way? Oh what a treat,
Each wrong turn is a new beat.

Embracing the Unfurling

Like a flower, petals sway,
Unraveling in a funny way.
Each bloom's a riddle, oh so bright,
We giggle at the strange delight.

Dancing with the breeze's tease,
Life's a game of 'if you please'.
Unfolding laughter, like a gift,
In the chaos, hearts will lift.

Stars in Unseen Skies

Under the clouds, a hidden show,
Twinkling secrets, all aglow.
On uncertain nights, we gaze above,
Finding smiles in the stars we love.

In the dark, our thoughts dive deep,
What's a leap if not a leap?
Starlit wishes, wild and free,
A whimsical dance of you and me.

Where Shadows Meet Light

In a world that's ever spinning,
Seeking answers without beginning,
Laughter's the bridge, not the fight,
Where shadows gleam, and hearts feel light.

Why fret about roads never taken?
The map's so torn, it must be fakin'.
Dance in the dark, forget the fright,
For shadows just long for some delight.

The Space Between Answers

In that gap where thoughts collide,
Most likely there's a joke inside.
Punchlines wait in the unknown,
Cracking smiles when we feel alone.

Questions float like paper boats,
Each one singing silly notes.
Sail on doubt, with laughter bright,
As we drift toward the daylight.

Chasing Illusions

Who needs the truth when dreams are near?
Illusions taste just like cold beer.
Chase the mirage, let happiness flow,
With laughter as wind, just let it go.

Reality's a tricky game,
Full of quirks and quite insane.
We'll trip and stumble, but that's alright,
For every fall brings quirky delight.

Wandering Without Destination

Stumbling through life, no final stop,
Like socks that find their way to pop.
Roaming free with no clear plan,
Even lost is just part of the fun.

Around each corner, surprises wait,
Life's buffet on a spinning plate.
Whimsical winds guide our flight,
In this dance of pure delight.

Flickers of the Unseen

In shadows we dance, oh what a sight,
With ghosts of our thoughts, we take flight.
Where socks disappear and keys like to hide,
We chuckle at life, with fate as our guide.

Like fireflies buzzing, they tickle our mind,
Each flicker a puzzle, bizarrely entwined.
We laugh at the chaos, it's part of the fun,
Finding joy in the mess, until day is done.

The Puzzle of Existence

Life's like a jigsaw missing some pieces,
With corners that vanish as laughter increases.
We search for connections, lost in the fray,
A cat in a box, who's just there to play.

With colors that clash and patterns that brawl,
We question our choices, and yet we stand tall.
The pieces are strange, some don't even fit,
But isn't it lovely, this whimsical bit?

Invitations to Explore

Step right up, dear friend, don't be shy,
Life offers tickets to a comedy sigh.
With maps full of scribbles, we wander in glee,
Finding joy in the wrong turns, oh can't you see?

The universe giggles at plans we enlace,
As we dance to the tunes of a cosmic embrace.
So grab your magnifier, and let's take a peek,
At mysteries laughing down each little creek.

Sailing on Uncharted Waters

A ship made of dreams, we set sail with a grin,
Navigating waves where the whimsy begins.
The compass is broken, but who needs a guide?
With laughter as wind, we bounce on the tide.

In storms of uncertainty, we raise up our cheers,
As dolphins join in, dissolving our fears.
Each splash tells a story, each wave is a dance,
So let's take the plunge, embrace the chance!

Reflections in a Glass Maze

In a maze made of glass, I wander and peep,
Hoping for answers, but just find a heap.
Reflections abound, all twisted and bent,
I laugh at the mirrors, what time they have spent.

A path that's unclear, each turn feels the same,
I stumble and giggle, this isn't a game.
With each step I take, I see another me,
A party of faces, a jumbled confetti.

The exit is lost, but who needs to flee?
I'll dance in this maze, and sip my green tea.
Embrace the confusion, it's all in good fun,
After all, life's chaos has barely begun.

Notes from the Edge of Uncertainty

Scribbles on napkins, some doodles and rhyme,
Notes from the edge; no sense of time.
I ponder the meaning of this wobbly chair,
While balancing snacks with a pigeon-like flair.

The road is a riddle, a curious quest,
I wave at each bump, they put me to test.
Like socks without partners, I'm lost in the fluff,
But laughter is currency, I've got more than enough.

I make small talk with clouds drifting by,
Ask them their secrets, they puff and they sigh.
They float with conviction, though rain might ensue,
So I pack up my dance and I'll shimmy askew.

The Timeless Drift

Time ticks away but I'm stuck in a loop,
A merry-go-round, with a very small troop.
I count all the seconds but lose track of days,
In this timeless drift, a quirkier phase.

I hum a sweet tune, while spinning about,
A dizzy delight, with nary a doubt.
I leap over puddles of thoughts on the run,
And skip through uncertainties, laughing just fun.

The clock has no power, it winks and it blinks,
As I scribble my thoughts in the space of drinks.
Join me and swagger, there's joy to unveil,
In this timeless drift, where chaos can sail.

Unraveling the Unexpected

I opened a box, what could I have found?
A sock puppet pirate, and a kazoo that's renowned.
Each twist in my day brings a laugh or a fight,
With shenanigans waiting around every night.

Plans made of jelly, they quiver and shake,
Just when I think, "Now, I'm heading for break!"
A banana peels out, and we slip in the fun,
Surprises are ripe, let's dance 'til we're done.

Life's a parade of the whacky, you see,
I gather my pals for a grand jamboree.
Through the twists of fate and the flips of the jest,
I find joy in the odd, because laughter's the best!

When Certainty Fades

When questions pile like laundry heaps,
And answers play hide and seek.
The GPS says, 'Just take a right,'
But the road's a twisty streak.

You throw the dice, they roll away,
Your fortune can't be bought.
Life's a game of 'pick a door,'
But all the prize is naught.

A map that shows where no one goes,
With landmarks like a chair.
You're destined for the great unknown,
Just make sure to beware.

So laugh as plans dissolve like smoke,
And dance in uncertainty.
For in the chaos, joy's involved,
Embrace delightful spree.

Threads of Ambiguity

In a world of tangled strings,
You pull just for the fun.
Each loop a question, answer late,
While chaos spins and runs.

The coffee spills a little strong,
Awake, you ponder 'why?'
Is this the start of something grand,
Or just a weird alibi?

With fortune cookies full of air,
You crack one for a laugh.
'You'll find your way — or maybe not,'
Oh, what a clever gaffe!

Take a breath and twirl around,
Dance in midst of doubt.
For in those threads of sticky glue,
You find what life's about.

The Beauty of Floating

Like a balloon that's lost its string,
You drift on whims of fate.
No anchor found, you bob along,
In circles small and great.

You paddle in a sea of dreams,
Where all directions blend.
A compass spun topsy-turvy,
Where will it lead, my friend?

The clouds above are fluffy thoughts,
That float and tease the mind.
Each wave a giggle at control,
As calmness gets maligned.

So let them sway, those thoughts of yours,
In gentle breezes' toss.
For floating free is truly grand,
And losing weight, not loss!

A Journey Without a Map

Step into shoes that squeak and squeal,
Wander with a grin that's wide.
No roadmap found, just follow fun,
Through fields of joy, you glide.

A signpost reads 'Maybe this way!'
As ducks cross streets in line.
With laughter echoing off the walls,
You stumble, drink, and dine.

The detours hold a myriad of sights,
Like ice cream spills and blobs.
With every twist of fate and luck,
You dodge the thorniest jobs.

So pack your bags of whimsy bright,
And off you dash with zest.
For life's a journey, come what may,
In wild and silly quest!

Dancing with Insecurity

In a world where questions roam,
I trip on my own two feet.
With every failed attempt I find,
I laugh at my own defeat.

The dance floor's full of 'what ifs',
I shuffle left, then check the door.
The rhythm's off, but who cares now?
I might just start a dance-off war.

A twirl of doubt, a spin of fate,
I wear my quirk like a crown.
With every fumble, I create,
A comedy, the world renowned.

So here I am, with laughter loud,
Insecurity, my jester friend.
We waltz through life as if it's grand,
And on this whim, we'll always blend.

The Tapestry of Trials

Life weaves tales of ups and downs,
Each thread a challenge, bright or bleak.
I stitch my doubts with tattered dreams,
And giggle at the ones I seek.

With needles sharp and fabric worn,
I patch the holes with silly plans.
The colors clash, but who is right?
My "masterpiece" is in the stands.

A tapestry of what could be,
With patterns wild, a crazy spree.
I make my worries into art,
Through laughter, life's not hard to see.

So if you stumble on my cloth,
Just laugh along, don't be dismayed.
For here's the stitch, the punchline bold:
In chaos, joy's serenade.

Echoes of the Unanswered

Echoes bounce off empty walls,
Questions linger in the air.
I shout my thoughts, they bounce and fade,
But laughter's found hiding there.

"Why am I here?" I start to muse,
And hear a giggle in reply.
The universe has jokes, you know,
It whispers truths as I comply.

In every conundrum, an odd twist,
An "aha!" moment, or maybe not.
I'll ponder deep while making tea,
Who knew that life was such a plot?

So when the echoes call my name,
I dawdle with a laugh or two.
For in the silence of my fears,
I find the humor that sees me through.

The Flickering Candle

A candle's light wobbles on stage,
On this journey, I'm but a flame.
As doubts swirl around with glee,
I giggle at my own silly game.

Each flicker hints at what's to come,
Will it dance or simply die?
In shadows long, I tell my fears,
While serving cake to Mister Why.

Wax drips down like time itself,
A sign of play or impending doom.
Yet laughter bubbles through the night,
As I embrace this candle's bloom.

So light a spark, and join the show,
For life's a flicker, yes indeed!
With humor masking every jest,
It's fun in every little deed.

The Sound of Silence

In quiet moments, I sit and stare,
Chasing thoughts that float through air.
A sock is lost, a shoe's astray,
Yet here I ponder, night and day.

The fridge hums softly, a ghostly tune,
I question life beneath the moon.
Is it the milk or the butter's dance?
Food for thought, or just a chance?

Laughing at cats that chase their tails,
While fish judge them from glassy gales.
The world is quirky, a vast parade,
Balloons and dreams that never fade.

In silence, wisdom comes like rain,
A drizzle soft, but never plain.
Grab a sandwich, join the fun,
Life's a picnic—let's not run!

Shadows that Whisper

Behind the curtain, shadows tease,
They dance and spin, they make us sneeze.
Why chase our fears, why fear the chase?
Life's just a game—let's play with grace.

I asked the mirror, "What do you see?"
It winked back, "Just you and me!"
Reflections share their bright delight,
While hiding from the blaring light.

The cat walks in, a royal stance,
Breaking my focus with an audacious glance.
Scratching the couch, a noble act,
Who knew chaos could be so exact?

Whispers echo in the mind,
In every corner, treasures we find.
Chasing shadows, grasping air,
Life's a riddle—who would care?

Tornadoes of Thought

A whirlwind spins inside my dome,
Thoughts zip around, they never roam.
Socks and sandwiches, all mixed in,
Am I winning, or did I sin?

Each spiral's a puzzle, a quirky test,
Am I the joke or just the jest?
Nonsense reigns in my busy head,
Where I embrace the unkempt thread.

Flying pies and peanut prayer,
Life's mayhem's sweet—a crazy affair.
Did I forget the recipe?
Here's a thought: let's just agree!

Like tornadoes, thoughts twist and spin,
A mix of chaos, that's where we begin.
So grab a slice of silly pie,
In this wild ride, we never die!

Paths Woven from Uncertainty

Wandering through the woods of thought,
I find the answers that I sought.
But then a squirrel interrupts my muse,
Chasing its tail, it skims to lose.

With every step, a fork appears,
Do I choose laughter, or face my fears?
Life's a map with lines that twist,
Each path leads to some funny tryst.

Uncertainty knocks with a knock so sly,
Wearing a hat and a bowtie high.
Joker or sage, you can't presume,
In this garden, all flowers bloom.

So here's my motto: let's skip and prance,
Embrace the wobble, lose the chance.
For in the chaos, joy will reign,
Our hearts weave threads through joyful pain!

Embracing the Unscripted

Life's a script with messy lines,
Characters dance, forget their signs.
Winging it is quite the art,
Chaotic joy, a silly start.

Plans like socks, they often mismatch,
We laugh and scratch, oh what a catch!
With every twist, there's room to play,
So let's embrace this wacky way.

Living in the Questions

Why's the sky blue? Who needs a map?
Questions tumble, a curious trap.
Seeking answers? What a ride!
Come join the fun, let doubts abide.

Is this cereal or a soup?
Life's conundrums, such a loop!
With every question, giggles grow,
Wonder is where the good things flow.

The Veil of Possibility

Behind a curtain, all could be,
What if chickens learned to ski?
Options flutter like a breeze,
In this theatre, we tease with ease.

A world of choices, so absurd,
Pigs can fly, have you heard?
So while we ponder, take a leap,
The magic's there, just dive deep.

The Labyrinth of Life

A maze of twists, turns, and glee,
Don't stress too much, just let it be.
Found a cat? It's part of the plan,
Ask it for directions, it's quite the fan!

With every corner, a squirrel may greet,
Dancing around, what a delightful feat!
Lost? Oh dear, but what's the harm?
Adventure calls, with its goofy charm.

Echoes in the Abyss

In the void where echoes play,
Thoughts bounce back, then slip away.
A sock gets lost, a shoe misplaced,
Reality's a humorous chase.

Waking up with dreams still here,
Coffee brewed, but thoughts unclear.
The cat stares at a dancing light,
Is it magic or sheer delight?

Time slips by, a sneaky thief,
Currently laughing at my grief.
A dance with fate, or maybe not,
I ponder while I forgot.

Life's a game of hide and seek,
Uncertainty gives luck a peek.
In the abyss, we roam and twirl,
Embracing chaos, give it a whirl.

The Fabric of Randomness

In a world of cozy threads,
Patterns woven, life is spread.
A sock with stripes, a shirt with dots,
Randomness ties all the knots.

When plans fall through like old balloons,
I laugh aloud, humming old tunes.
The universe winks with a twist,
In fabric's dance, it's hard to resist.

Do we wear our fate like a hat?
Or skip around like a playful cat?
Unraveled yarn, a tangled skein,
Who knew chaos could bring us gain?

Embrace the threads that life supplies,
Funny how serendipity flies.
With every stitch, a story glows,
In the warp and weft, we know.

Steps in the Dark

Cautious footsteps in pitch-black night,
Count to ten, then brave the fright.
Stubbing toes on pieces of fate,
Hard to dance when lost but great!

Echoes whisper, 'Don't trip, my friend!'
While shadows giggle, they never end.
A cryptic laugh, in silence profound,
Where missteps lead to joy unbound.

Searching for light like ducks in row,
Twisting paths, what do we know?
In funny struts, we find our way,
In darkness, we'll still seize the day.

Each step a riddle, a grand charade,
Who needs a map when fun's made?
Embrace the unknown and let it spark,
Life's dance is better when it's dark.

Tides of Ambivalence

Riding waves of what could be,
Highs and lows, a fickle sea.
Flip a coin, the fate is set,
Sailing ships with little debt.

Springtime sun or winter's chill,
Do we dive, or just sit still?
Surfing questions with no clear shore,
Where will the laughter lead us more?

The tide rolls in with a chuckle bright,
Paddling hard, then feeling light.
A quirky dance, a carefree spin,
Wave upon wave, let the fun begin!

As we float on this sea of chance,
Life throws a punch; we laugh, we prance.
With each big splash, we learn to say,
Embrace the tide, come what may!

The Paradox of the Untold Journey

I set my feet on roads unknown,
With every step, my mind has grown.
Yet as I march, my thoughts get stuck,
In the odd dance of dumb old luck.

The closer I get, the farther I roam,
In a land that's weird, away from home.
Maps are just drawings that laugh at me,
Waving their hands like, 'Just wait and see!'

I trip on thoughts, I stumble on dreams,
Plotting my course while bursting at seams.
A guide who's lost, with no firm plan,
Running in circles, still calls it a 'ban'.

But oh, what fun! The laughs break free,
Life's a road trip—just you and me.
So grab your snacks, and don't forget drinks,
We're settling in for our wildest thinks.

Searching for Stars in the Daylight

Oh, where are the stars when the sun is bright?
I squint and search with all my might.
They hide behind clouds, or maybe in dreams,
A cosmic game with baffling schemes.

Up in the sky, all I see is blue,
While gravity's got me stuck like glue.
I gaze at my shadow and give it a wink,
It's out there stargazing; don't you think?

Maybe they wait for the dusk to dance,
Or hide in the day with a clever stance.
I'll catch one soon—just wait, you see?
With a giant net made of cheese and glee.

So here I stand, with a grin so bright,
Hunting for stars in this silly light.
The universe chuckles; it's all in jest,
Life's a riddle—a hilarious quest!

Threadbare Dreams in the Twilight

In that soft glow where day meets night,
Dreams wear thin but still hold tight.
I tell them tales with laughter and tears,
They giggle back, revealing my fears.

A frayed old quilt of hopes once grand,
Stitched with stories, too tight to stand.
They wobble and sway as the daylight fades,
Making odd shapes in the twilight glades.

I shout to the dreams, 'Why so cliché?'
They roll their eyes, 'We're here to stay!'
In comic relief, they tease and brawl,
Like clowns juggled in a neon hall.

And as the stars blink into sight,
Threadbare dreams shine with all their might.
Though worn and tattered, they dance in glee,
Reminding me life's a grand parody.

Lessons from the Cracked Mirror

I gazed at myself in a mirror so cracked,
Reflections scrambled, but laughter intact.
It shows a jester in peculiar frames,
With hair like a crow and my worst of aims.

Each shard reflects a truth askew,
A joker's take; who knew it was you?
I wave at the chaos, we laugh in glee,
Life's a comedy, come share a tea!

Imperfections burst forth like wild balloons,
Teaching me wisdom, between the tunes.
"Embrace the mess!" the reflections cheer,
"Life's just a circus, now grab a beer!"

So every crack holds a giggle and two,
A spot to dance, a glimpse of the new.
In the mirror's fate, may chaos unfurl,
Life's most brilliant—when twirled like a whirl.

The Compass of Doubt

Lost in a maze of choices,
Each turn quakes with surprise.
Should I wear blue or green socks?
Life's too short for dull ties.

Maps that lead to nowhere fast,
I wander with a frown,
Directions scribbled in crayon,
That's how I get around.

Pondering frozen pizza,
Or a gourmet dish that's grand,
One's a dinner for a king,
The other feeds a band.

Yet in the haze of blunders,
We're all a bit askew,
At least my socks match nicely,
Even if my path is blue.

Serendipity in the Shadows

Stumbling upon lost treasures,
Like keys for a locked door.
Cacti that blossom like parties,
Who knew smart plants could score?

In a world of tangled luck,
I tripped on my own feet,
Found a fortune in the chaos,
Riding on my heartbeat.

Miracles hide in corners,
Like socks that make a team,
Jumping out from closets,
To play in my daydream.

Embrace the wild detours,
Even clowns can be profound,
When shadows dance with laughter,
Joy's waiting to be found.

Dance of the Unpredictable

Waltzing with uncertainty,
Two left feet on my quest.
Life shuffles like a DJ,
Each beat's a surprise test.

Jumping when the music stops,
Jack-in-the-box delight,
You never know what's coming next,
Until you hear the flight.

Twists and turns of fate's own tune,
Make room for silly spins,
With laughter as my partner here,
Life's a game that wins.

So grab your shoes and follow me,
Forget the missed step's dread,
In dances of the crazy worn,
We twirl until we're fed.

The Art of Letting Go

Clearing clutter from my mind,
Like dust from an old chest.
I toss the plans I held so tight,
To free my soul for rest.

Life's a game of catch and release,
With balls that rarely land,
I throw my hopes into the breeze,
Time slips right from my hand.

Turning worries into bubbles,
And watching them just pop,
Freeing dreams on windy days,
Like ice cream from the shop.

Embracing chaos with a grin,
Uncertainty's my flair,
With a wink and a wave goodbye,
I dance without a care.

The Delicate Balance of Maybe

In the morning I woke up late,
Should I eat or just procrastinate?
A dance with toast, a waltz with tea,
Maybe or maybe not, oh glee!

The cat stretched wide, the dog just snores,
Should I check my email or explore?
A sock on the floor calls out my name,
To sort or not? It's all just the same!

Flip a coin, let chance take the wheel,
Should I ask, "How do you feel?"
The universe chuckles, a wink so sly,
Decisions are just a burger fry!

In the end, it's the laugh we chase,
In chaos and choice, we find our place.
So here's to the maybes, both big and small,
Life's just a game, let's have a ball!

Serendipity in the Chaotic Flow

I lost my keys, oh what a mess,
Did I check the fridge, or call my ex?
The world spins round, like a playful twirl,
Serendipity whispers, "Give it a whirl!"

Stumbled on laughter in a coffee shop,
With a latte mustache, I simply can't stop.
A wrong turn led me to the best of pizza,
Sometimes life's a trippy little fiesta!

Mismatched socks, my weekend attire,
In a maze of choices, I never tire.
A dance of fate, a skip of cheer,
The chaos is fun, let's make it clear!

Unexpected joy greets me each day,
With goofy moments that come out to play.
Serendipity, oh what a guide,
In this weird world's wacky ride!

A Kaleidoscope of Questioning Souls

Am I a lion or just a cat?
In the mirror's grin, imagine that!
Today I asked, 'What's my plan?'
The mirror laughed, said, "Be the fan!"

With colors swirling, life's a spree,
Should I juggle or just sip my tea?
Questions pop like popcorn kernels,
In the movie of life, we twist like twirls.

Is rain a tear or nature's glee?
I can't decide, it's all just free!
Life's a puzzle, missing a piece,
In the chase for answers, let laughter increase!

A kaleidoscope spins tales untold,
As wisdom flickers, both warm and cold.
With silly queries, we dance through time,
In the circus of life, let's paint it sublime!

The Weight of Unsung Answers

In the attic of thoughts, dust bunnies roam,
Unsung answers feel far from home.
Should I dig deep or just let it be?
Will the elusive answer ever agree?

A question is like socks after the wash,
Mismatched, but hey—it's all posh!
Life's quirky riddles, each a tease,
I searched for the right one, just with ease.

The scales tipped with every ponder,
Should I leap or just sit and wander?
In the quest for truth, we laugh and sigh,
With questions aplenty, we'll give it a try!

So here's to the weight we carry each day,
In silence and chaos, we find our way.
With unsung answers, we dance and play,
In this waltz of wonder, come what may!

The Kaleidoscope of Life

Life spins like a wheel, oh what a sight,
Colors clash and play, both day and night.
We stumble through puzzles, both big and small,
With laughter as our guide, we can conquer all.

Jellybeans of joy, and licorice regrets,
Twisting through chaos, we make no bets.
Like juggling cats in a three-ring show,
We wiggle and giggle, just go with the flow.

Dancing on rainbows, we giggle with glee,
Unraveling each knot, sipping herbal tea.
We can't find the map, but we've got our charm,
In this wacky adventure, we mean no harm.

So embrace the wild ride, with all of its bends,
Each turn brings us closer, to more quirky friends.
With a wink and a nod, we'll figure it out,
Life's a grand circus; let's cheer and shout!

Moments in the Mist

In foggy confusion, we stumble and trip,
Seeking clarity like an ill-fated ship.
Each moment a puzzle, a riddle we face,
We laugh at our woes, in this peculiar race.

The mist hides our doubts, like socks in the wash,
While we search for the path, feeling quite posh.
Like ducks in a row, we quack on ahead,
With giggles and hiccups, we're joyfully led.

With every misstep, we dance with delight,
As shadows play tricks, through the day and night.
We chase after dreams, like a feather on air,
Finding fun in the fog, with nary a care.

So let's wander through mists, hand in hand,
Bounding over puddles, as we make our stand.
Life's a whimsical blur, let's not miss a beat,
In every moment of fog, it's joy we will meet!

Sculpting Dreams from Shadows

In the dim-lit corners, our dreams come to play,
Sculpting odd shapes, like distortions at bay.
With a twist of our thoughts, and a flick of our hands,
We carve out our wishes from whimsical sands.

Shadows might linger, with whispers so sly,
Dancing and prancing, like glimmers that fly.
We chuckle at shadows, big and quite small,
With laughter, they shrink, or dare we say, fall?

Each figure we mold, from silliness born,
Is a testament, dear friends, we're never forlorn.
With chisel of humor, we chip away doubt,
In a world full of shadows, we twist and shout.

So grab your clay dreams, don't let them decay,
Let's sculpt the night's humor, in a joyous array.
From shadows to brilliance, we'll spin tales anew,
Life's an art gallery, and you're the debut!

Finding Clarity in the Confusion

In a whirlwind of thoughts, we dizzy and swirl,
Like a bee in a bonnet, with a playful twirl.
We fumble and fidget, with smiles on our face,
In the land of confusion, let's quicken our pace.

With pockets of nonsense, we wander and roam,
Searching for clarity in this befuddled home.
Each question a duck, quacking loud in the air,
But laughter is the secret, that lightens our care.

Through the maze of our minds, we skip and we hop,
Like bunnies on trampolines, we bounce and don't stop.
As the fog lifts away, like a magician's show,
We giggle at answers, we thought we'd never know.

So let's skip in confusion, with glee in our hearts,
In this big jumbled puzzle, each moment imparts.
With joy as our compass, we'll navigate bright,
Finding clarity in chaos, it's always in sight!

Embracing the Unraveled Thread

In a world where cheese does roll,
I question my very soul.
Should I stand or take that leap?
Maybe pierce that doubts we keep.

With socks that don't ever match,
Is it chaos or a scratch?
Spilled coffee on the clean white sheet,
It's life's odd little treat.

I trip on thoughts, they laugh and coil,
Like spaghetti left to boil.
Do I dance, or do I fall?
More fun to just embrace it all.

So I twirl around the mess,
With gum stuck on my dress.
Life's twists wrap round my head,
Hooray for fabric, unsewn thread!

Echoes in the Abyss

In the dark, I hear a cheer,
Is it doubt, or my missing beer?
Whispers of choices that slip and slide,
Tarzan swinging, no place to hide.

The abyss calls, it yawns so wide,
Should I dance or take a ride?
Echoes bounce from wall to wall,
Maybe I'll just heed the call.

Banana peels underfoot,
Do I run or do I scoot?
Life's a joke, wrapped in a jest,
Who knew chaos was the best?

A leap of faith, or grab a snack?
On this path, there's no way back.
I laugh with shadows and embrace the fizz,
In this throw of dice, I dance like a whiz.

The Art of Wandering Aimlessly

With no map and mismatched shoes,
I wonder why I have these blues.
Each street I turn leads to nowhere,
But look! A cat has some flair!

With no destination on my mind,
I find jewels of the curious kind.
A stranger's smile, a pizza slice,
Who knew life's randomness is so nice?

In narrow alleys, I lose my way,
Who needs plans for another day?
Life is like a game of chess,
Except the queen's in a funky dress.

So throw the map, let whims decide,
Life's awkward dance is quite a ride.
Through chaos and laughter, I wander free,
Without that point, I just might be me!

When Certainty Takes Flight

Like pigeons on a windy spree,
Certainty flees, oh woe is me!
I chase a dream that's lost in clouds,
While tripping over laughing crowds.

With plans that swell like a balloon,
A pop! And it ends all too soon.
Do I try to soar or stay right here?
I sip my tea with some fear.

Chasing rainbows, dodging fate,
Do I hesitate, or contemplate?
Logic slips and giggles escape,
Who knew life's a silly shape?

So, when the compass spins and wobbles,
And inner voices make me dawdle,
I spread my wings, embrace the shift,
In uncertainty, I find my gift!

The Journey Through Chaos

Waking up to socks that don't match,
Coffee spills as I make a quick catch.
The map says left, but it's really a right,
Chaos in jeans, but I'll be alright.

The roads twist like spaghetti on plates,
Traffic's a puzzle, but I love my fates.
A detour to ice cream, how could I resist?
Life's a wildcard, and I make a list!

A bird on my shoulder, singing a tune,
Whispers of wisdom under the moon.
Laughter erupts from a tree on my street,
In chaos, I dance to my own silly beat.

So here's to the bumps and unexpected turns,
Each misstep gives way to the joy that I earn.
With a laugh and a twirl, I'll embrace the spree,
In this wild journey, I'll always be free.

Seeds of Uncertainty

Planting my doubts in a whimsical plot,
Watering worries, what's brewing? A lot!
Each seed could sprout giggles or frowns,
In the garden of chaos, I dance with the clowns.

Sunshine and rain, they both come, it's true,
Why stress the forecast when I can just brew?
A salad of mishaps, let's toss it around,
Flavor of laughter is where joy is found.

Weeds in my thoughts? Just make them a show,
A parade of uncertainty twirls to and fro.
Digging for meaning, I stumble and trip,
Sprouting absurdity, I'll take a big sip!

So here's to the seeds planted wild in my mind,
Each day a funny plot twist I find.
With a wink and a smile, let's grow all we can,
In the garden of life, I'm the jester, the fan.

A Story Untold

In the attic of chance, dusty tales lie,
I trip on the stories that somehow went by.
Gathering moments like kites in the air,
What's next on this ride? I haven't a care!

A cat in a top hat seems quite out of place,
And yet he insists there's a party to grace.
With laughter as my compass, we follow the sound,
Chasing the threads of the joys that abound.

A mishap with words, I stutter and fumble,
But the crowd bursts with laughter, and I just feel humble.

Each stumble's a step towards a tale that's more grand,
Making memories sticky, like gloves covered in sand.

So here's to the stories we weave as we roam,
In the chaos and giggles, we find a new home.
With each twist of fate and every road toll,
I dance through the chapters; it's how I roll!

The Journey of Questions

Why do ducks wear tiny shoes?
Is it to avoid muddy blues?
What keeps the sun from taking a dive?
Or do ice cream trucks really drive?

Is it the socks that inspire our dreams?
Or the way that laughter softly beams?
Why does the cat stare at the wall?
Is she waiting for her next big call?

Do clouds ever tire of floating high?
Do they wonder how it feels to fly?
With all this questioning in the air,
Will my socks ever find their pair?

So let's laugh at the things we ask,
Embrace the puzzle, it's quite the task.
Life's a riddle in a funny disguise,
With answers hidden in our own skies.

Labyrinths of the Mind

In the maze of thoughts, who's in charge?
Is it the goldfish or an oversized barge?
What's that noise that never seems clear?
Could it be wisdom or just my ear?

A creeping question, oh, where does it lead?
Do I follow the rabbit or pick up speed?
Should I wear mismatched socks for a change?
Or just claim my routine as a bit strange?

The walls start to giggle, they're such a tease,
Maybe I'm lost, or maybe I'm free.
Do I need a map, or just a snack?
Oh look, there's a squirrel in a top hat!

With humor as my guide and a heart full of cheer,
I'll wander this labyrinth without any fear.
Every twist, every turn just adds to my fun,
Let's skip through the questions until I can run!

The Heart's Compass

Does the heart know where to go?
Is it wise, or just a little slow?
Should I follow the beat or take a rest?
Does it know what makes me feel blessed?

When the world feels round and quite mad,
Do we laugh at the good and embrace the bad?
Can love be a compass in chaos' way?
Or should I just nap for the rest of the day?

Each pulse a question like footsteps in sand,
Are they leading me somewhere just as planned?
With a wink to jest and a nod to the fun,
Can life really progress when we run and run?

So here's to the heart's silly dance,
Finding joy in each wobbly chance.
Even when lost, we'll never relent,
For the journey's the joke, and we are the jest!

Pages Yet to be Written

Is my story a drama or a comedy spree?
Will the plot twist in ways yet to be?
With blank pages ready, my pen at the side,
I'll scribble my heart, with nothing to hide.

What if I wrote of bananas that sing?
Or painted a dragon with a sparkly ring?
Shall I dwell on the mundane or dive into cheer?
When every tick-tock might disappear?

Though uncertainty looms like a looming shadow,
I'll craft my tale beneath bright and shallow.
Will my characters laugh, or will they just sigh?
With a wink and a nudge, we'll learn to fly!

So here's to the chapters, unwritten and bold,
Replete with my laughter, in each verse of gold.
Life's just a book where the fun never ends,
Let's write it with glitter and giggles, my friends!

The Silence Between the Lines

In a world full of chatter, we ponder and play,
Yet silence speaks louder, in its own funny way.
With questions like bubbles, we chase them around,
As laughter erupts in the lost and the found.

Wording our worries with giggles and grins,
Finding the humor in life's little spins.
The lines that connect us can twist and can bend,
A comedy sketch that has no clear end.

We dance through the doubts like it's just a routine,
Dropping our worries in the spaces between.
The punchline of living, it's rarely so clear,
But laughter's the ticket to not disappear.

So here's to the whispers that tickle our hearts,
To the giggles and wiggles, life's glorious arts.
In the silence that teases, let courage arise,
As we laugh at the seems, 'til it's time for goodbyes.

Fleeting Certainties

Like clouds in the sky, all fluffy and bright,
The certainties drift, escaping our sight.
We grab at them swiftly, and then they just fly,
Leaving us puzzled, as we heave a sigh.

One moment we're gardeners, planting our dreams,
The next we're stuck asking, or so it seems.
With hopes that are bouncing like balls off a wall,
Finding joy in the chaos, we giggle and sprawl.

The maps that we follow can lead us astray,
Yet we stumble through life in a joyful ballet.
With hats on our heads and our shoes mismatched,
A dance of uncertainty—who's really attached?

So let's toast to the whims, the tumble and roll,
To fleeting certainties that take on a toll.
In the vast unknown, we trip, laugh, and twirl,
For the beauty of life is in the swirl.

The Unraveled Narrative

A story once woven, now unraveled with glee,
Plot twists and mishaps, like a farce on TV.
Characters mingle, both quirky and bold,
As laughter aligns with the chaos untold.

In chapters of blunders, we scribble and scrawl,
The pages of humor, oh they hold us all.
With metaphors dancing like socks on the floor,
We tickle our fancies till our sides roar.

The climax eludes us, but we cannot complain,
For the comedy lies in the bends of the lane.
The arcs that we travel can twist and can break,
Yet we laugh at the follies that we cannot shake.

So here's to the script that's a riot of fun,
To the unraveled tale where we all come undone.
In the book of our lives, let's scribble with flair,
As we pen our adventures with laughter to share.

Beyond the Horizon of Knowing

There's a land far from here, where the answers run free,
But the path is a riddle, as tricky as can be.
With signs pointing left, and a sun in our eyes,
We wander in circles 'til we finally rise.

With maps made of giggles and compasses cracked,
We venture onward, though often way off track.
In the land of 'what if' and 'maybe' galore,
The humor of life becomes hard to ignore.

So let's skip past the borders of rigid and clear,
To the places where questions are paired with a cheer.
We'll laugh through the fog, in the dance of the day,
Finding joy in the mystery that leads us astray.

Beyond the horizon, where knowing is vague,
We chase all the giggles as life waxes and fades.
In the light of the unknown, we'll raise up our glass,
To the riddles of life—come join for the laugh!

The Tethered Compass

My compass spins, oh what a sight,
It points to dinner, what a delight!
North is for those who stay in line,
But I'll head west for pizza and wine.

The map's outdated, with burritos galore,
Yet here I stand at a locked-bathroom door.
"Is this the way to happiness, dear?"
I ask my dog, who wags with cheer.

With every twist and every turn,
I laugh at lessons I'll never learn.
The stars above just giggle and shine,
As I wander the paths that I design.

So sway along with life's silly beat,
Where plans are scribbles, fading neat.
Adventure's a word with slippery flair,
Find joy in the mayhem, if you dare!

Shadows of the Unknown

In the dark, there are monsters, or so they say,
But maybe it's just a bear in dismay.
"Too much ice cream!" he grumbles with fright,
"Why did I think I could dance through the night?"

The shadows giggle, a mischievous crew,
"Why fret on the choices? Just try something new!"
Like socks with sandals, or fruit on a pie,
In the world of chaos, let your spirit fly.

With every decision, I trip and I sway,
Who knew getting lost could brighten the day?
I dance with the goblins and trip on a shoe,
Life is absurd, but isn't it true?

So smile at the things you cannot control,
For what is life without some comic roll?
A twirl, a laugh, like clouds in the sky,
In shadows of doubt, just let yourself fly!

Dancing on the Edge of Doubt

I stand on tiptoes, a wobbly leap,
Will I fall down? Well, I'm not losing sleep.
The ground looks inviting, a soft, grand bed,
But if I jump, will I just bump my head?

Life's a dance in clumsy shoes,
With moves that make you sing the blues.
Just when you think you've found your groove,
A rug gets pulled, you gotta move!

"Should I sign that form?" my brain whirls about,
"Or should I just dance on the edge of doubt?"
With a laugh and a shimmy, I shout "Let's go!"
It doesn't really matter; just trust the flow.

In uncertain steps, it's easy to fall,
But the best stories come from a stumble or sprawl.
So take my hand, let's frolic and shout,
It's all just a dance on the edge of doubt!

A Map of Fleeting Moments

I unfold my map, filled with trails of glee,
Where ice cream mountains await you and me.
A X marks the spot where we lost our way,
Chasing after clouds, and night turned to day.

Each moment a color, a splash, and a cheer,
Filled with laughter, and perhaps a few tears.
I search for the moments that slip through the cracks,
Like socks in the dryer, they never come back!

So draw me a line, ink it with joy,
Mix it with sunshine, and a sprinkle of coy.
For all that we seek is a fleeting embrace,
In a world where the map can't keep up with pace.

Let's navigate life with a wink and a grin,
With all of our quirks and the chaos within.
For in every corner, there's magic to find,
A map of our moments, though tangled and blind!

Rooms Without Doors

In a room with no doors, I took a seat,
Wondering how I'll ever meet,
The snacks on the table, they've vanished,
Did I eat them or lose my own sandwich?

I ticked off the boxes of life's silly lists,
But all I found were some unmade twists,
The lightbulb is buzzing, and so is my brain,
If unplanned is the pathway, let's dance in the rain.

I look for an exit, but end up with puns,
Jokes on myself, oh life's twisted runs,
Who knew that one could get stuck with the woes,
In rooms with no doors, just riddles and prose?

So toast to confusion, a clumsy ballet,
I'll trip over laughter, let chaos hold sway,
With frolicsome thoughts and a grin, my dear,
Here's to life's mystery, let's give it a cheer!

Conversations with Doubt

Doubt sat beside me, a chatty old crow,
Telling me secrets, and we laughed at the flow,
'You think life has answers? Oh, young naive!'
I chuckled right back, 'Let's just misbehave!'

We pondered on choices, the paths that we take,
Flipping coins wildly, for good luck's sake,
'What if I leap?' I asked with a grin,
Doubt said with a wink, 'Just see where you spin!'

Each question's a puzzle, wrapped up in a tease,
Doubt offered solutions, just one, maybe three,
'Life's filled with odd turns, with capers and clowns,
So, jump into whimsy, leave logic in frowns!'

As the sun dipped down, we shared a last laugh,
Doubt nodded, it loved the absurd little path,
With a wave of its wing, it flitted away,
Leaving me chuckling, what a fine day!

The Interlude of Mystery

Oh, life's a stage with a twist in the play,
Where scenes switch suddenly, come what may,
I learned to dance with the fog and the haze,
As questions like fireflies flicker and blaze.

In the middle of nowhere, I found a lost sock,
I asked it for wisdom; it just ticked like a clock,
'You see, dear friend, I'm fetching some flair,
Sometimes the finest is hiding, I swear!'

With a wink and a nod, the sock gave me glee,
Twirled off to the left, went beyond a tall tree,
I'll follow its trail, in this quirky ballet,
For life's full of mysteries, hip-hip-hooray!

So let's laugh at the unknown, embrace the bizarre,
Each detour a story, each sigh a wild star,
In the interlude of all that we seek,
Let's paint our own canvas, let joy be our peak!

Unfolding the Unfathomable

In the land of the lost, I opened my mind,
To unravel the roots of the puzzling kind,
A riddle appeared, with a giggle and flair,
Saying, 'Solve me, dear friend, if you dare!'

I scratched at my head, and a thought bumped my brain,
Should I be serious or dance in the rain?
The unfathomable whispered sweet cheeky tunes,
While I taped up my daydreams with glittery spoons.

With a jolt of confusion, I flipped through my notes,
Found banana peels under wise, old goats,
Each twist and each turn was a jest in disguise,
Wrapping up laughter in colourful lies.

So raise up your glass to the strange and the odd,
To the jests of the heart, to the whimsy of God,
In folding the layers of life's wacky play,
Let's revel in chaos, hip-hip-hooray!

Reveries of the Unexplored Mind

Dreams bubble up like soda pop,
Wonders waiting just to drop.
A thought so wild it spins and twirls,
In the realm of boys and girls.

Ideas dance like socks in piles,
Tangled up in goofy smiles.
Should I wear the red or the blue?
Oh dear, I forgot my shoe!

In this maze of bright balloons,
Laughter echoes, silly tunes.
I chase my thoughts both near and far,
While sipping tea from a candy jar.

So ponder freely, do not fret,
Life's a comedy, I'd place a bet!
With twists and turns round every bend,
The punchline's near, just wait, my friend!

Navigating the Fog

Through the mist, I squint and strain,
Hoping for sunshine like it's a game.
But fog is thick, like my auntie's stew,
Is that a tree, or a raccoon too?

I wander aimlessly with a grin,
Stumbling on a great big win!
A fallen branch or maybe bliss,
Oh wait, no, just a bee that missed.

Navigating life's tangled strands,
Arms out wide, I make my plans.
A little dance, a hop, a skip,
Dodging life's existential trip!

Through twilight's twirl, I'll find my way,
With silly thoughts to save the day.
In every step, there's fun to claim,
In this grand, odd, uncertain game!

The Many Faces of Chaos

In a world of socks that do not match,
I tiptoe cautiously, oh, what a catch!
The cat's up high, trying to take flight,
While I just hope to avoid a bite.

Chaos, dear friend, wears many hats,
Donning smiles, grumpy frowns, and silly spats.
It's like a puzzle missing a piece,
Yet every moment brings new release.

With a burst of fun, like popcorn pop,
I juggle worries, flip and flop.
A mighty dance amidst the mess,
Learning that chaos is just a guess!

So laugh at the whirlwind's silly spin,
Embrace the comedy deep within.
For in this chaos, we all reside,
Together laughing on this ride!

Embracing the Unknown

In the shadows where wonders creep,
Lies a scoop of joy, or so I leap!
Mysteries hide like peek-a-boo,
What's there waiting? A llama? A shoe?

I paddle boats on a lake of dreams,
With rubber ducks and a wallet of creams.
Each turn of fate a freaky show,
Sailing along where no one knows.

A treasure map scribbled by hand,
Leading to giggles in a far-off land.
When life gets sketchy, take the dive,
Who knows what fun might come alive!

So I'll embrace the quirks and the freaks,
With questions aplenty and silly peaks.
For in this unknown, my heart will sing,
As I dance in circles, a foolish king!

Navigating Through the Fog

In a world so bright, where's the map?
I stumble forward, and hear a clap.
A GPS? Nah, just my nose in a sneeze,
When life gets foggy, it's best to tease.

Clouds roll in, and I greet the rain,
With laughter and joy, who needs the pain?
A compass spinning, I dance in confusion,
This wild confusion? A grand illusion!

Through the haze, I see a light,
A beacon of hope, or a raccoon fight?
I cheer for the maybes, the whys that are free,
In this foggy journey, just let it be!

So here's to the fun of the lost and the found,
In the mist of life, let's spin around.
With every misstep, let's jump and play,
For in the fog, we'll find our way!

The Beauty of Unfinished Tales

A story starts with a line or two,
But ends with a hiccup, what else is new?
Characters wander, and plot twists abound,
In this messy novel, laughter is found.

They say life's scripted, but who wrote this play?
I'd like to know, so I can have my say.
With cliffhangers lingering, oh what a tease,
Unfinished tales can come with some ease.

Turning the page—oops, what's that smell?
A pizza burning? Or do I dwell?
The beauty of scribbles on the wrinkled page,
Is knowing it's perfect, no need for a sage.

So let's raise a glass to the dangling threads,
To unfinished tales, and unspoken spreads.
In every odd chapter, may laughter prevail,
Let's giggle and wiggle through life's crazy gale!

Uncharted Paths of the Heart

With a map that's missing, I wander astray,
My heart's GPS? It's gone out to play.
Each twist and turn is a prankster's delight,
In uncharted pathways, I relish the fright.

Well-meaning friends say, "Follow your bliss!"
But how do I find it? I seem to miss.
With every wrong turn, I discover a gem,
Life's hidden treasures—they're all just a whim!

The road less traveled is bumpy and wild,
Reminds me of being an unsure child.
But giggles emerge from the places I roam,
In these uncharted paths, I'm never alone.

With each little stumble, my heart skips a beat,
The joy of the journey—so bittersweet.
So let's frolic together, make messy art,
In uncharted paths, lies the fun of the heart!

Whispers of a Wavering Mind

Thoughts dance around like fireflies at night,
One says, "Keep calm!" while the other takes flight.
A nagging question, like a tickling bug,
My mind's a soft pillow, but also a rug.

"Do I like this pizza?" I ponder aloud,
While chaos erupts, like I'm lost in a crowd.
Thoughts in a riddle, a tangled-up mess,
In the land of wobble, I often digress.

The whispers giggle, a chorus absurd,
Each tiny doubt becomes a loud bird.
I laugh at the chatter, so totally kismet,
In my wavering mind, who needs a sure bet?

So let's toast to thoughts that never align,
To the funny whispers that dance like fine wine.
In this swirling journey, let's shrug and unwind,
Embrace the madness, whispers of the mind!

Building Sandcastles

In the sun we shape our dreams,
With cups and buckets, silly schemes.
The tide comes in, we laugh and shout,
'Is this what life's really about?'

A castle grand, it's built so high,
Then washed away, oh my, oh my!
We giggle as we scramble quick,
To build again, it's quite the trick!

But out of sand, we make our stand,
With seashell windows, quite unplanned.
We wave our flags of laughter bright,
In this fine mess, we feel delight!

So here's to castles, made in jest,
Life's fleeting moments, we're truly blessed.
With every wave, we dance and play,
Tomorrow's tide will sweep away.

The Path Less Traveled

Two paths diverged in woods so green,
One's paved in gold, the other unseen.
I chose the one with dust and grime,
A shortcut's worth, or just a crime?

I tripped on roots and tumbled down,
My hopes and dreams, they wore a frown.
But through the bushes, laughter peeks,
The best of plans are quite the freaks!

So here I am, so lost and found,
A merry dance on shaky ground.
With every wrong turn that I take,
I find the joy that's hard to fake!

So let's embrace this winding trail,
With snacks and jokes, we'll never fail.
For in the mess, we find the cheer,
The path less traveled, oh so dear!

A Symphony of Questions

What's that sound? Is it a tune?
Or just my brain, with thoughts to swoon?
Each question forms a note so bold,
A symphony, or so I'm told.

Chopsticks played on pots and pans,
Conducted by my clumsy hands.
The audience? Just my cat's stare,
Wondering if I'm quite all there.

With every query, an echo rings,
Why's the bird in the moonlight sings?
I search for answers, but I find,
The joy is in the curious mind!

So join my band of quirky quests,
Let's dance in chaos, life's the best!
In questions, laughter, and the fun,
We make sweet music till we're done!

Between Possibility and Reality

In dreams, I'm flying, oh what a sight!
But then I trip over a shoelace tight.
Between the stars and my tiny bed,
Are chances for laughter, joy, and dread.

Reality's here with its boring trends,
While possibility's dancing, making amends.
I juggle both like a circus clown,
Is it thrilling up, or am I just down?

With open arms, I reach for it all,
A dance on the line, waiting to fall.
Between two worlds, I swerve and sway,
It's all a game, let's play, hooray!

So here I stand, a balance to keep,
With dreams so wild and secrets deep.
A giggle, a grin, as I twist in the breeze,
Between my hopes and this life's unease!

Not Quite Arriving

I packed my bags, the map in hand,
But every road led to quicksand.
I found a detour, or maybe two,
Got lost in thought, as lost boys do.

I checked my watch, it ticked away,
Waited for guidance from the freeway.
But GPS said with great delight,
"Just make a left, then drift at night!"

A pizza place caught my wandering eye,
I ordered deep-fried doubts on the side.
The waiter winked, said with a grin,
"The secret's here, just dive right in!"

So here I stand at a forked road,
With a sundae brain and a traffic code.
Is it about arriving, or just the ride?
I'll giggle and snack, I'm full of pride!

The Path of Ambivalence

I asked a sage, or was it a frog?
He croaked and leapt right into the bog.
"Should I stay, or should I go?"
He grinned and said, "It's all for show!"

In the swirl of choices, I feel so wise,
Yet every answer wears a disguise.
A yes, a no, both feel so dull,
Perhaps ice cream is the way to pull!

Every step forward feels like a dance,
Stumbling over my own silly chance.
Do I wear shoes, or just my flaws?
The universe simply shrugs and yawns.

So wade through the waters of this unsure fate,
With laughter and snacks on the plate.
Life's an adventure, a grand charade,
Ambivalence? Just a joke well played!

Fleeting Moments of Clarity

I had an epiphany just last week,
While sipping coffee that tasted bleak.
It vanished fast, like socks in the wash,
Leaving me puzzled, and feeling posh.

In a world of chaos, I found a rhyme,
That made me chuckle, lost track of time.
The secrets of life, I thought I spied,
But they slipped away when I opened wide.

A squirrel with wisdom, or so I thought,
Left me pondering lessons he bought.
"Keep chasing dreams," he chattered away,
"But don't forget snacks at the end of the day!"

Glancing at wisdom, I often just grin,
In fleeting moments when chaos spins.
So here's to the laughter, both real and clear,
In an uncertain dance, let's spread some cheer!

The Canvas of Tomorrow

With brushes of doubt, I paint my fate,
Each stroke a question, each line a wait.
Colors of hope in a palette askew,
A wild masterpiece that's still coming through.

I splatter my dreams with giggles and glee,
And dance with the shadows that won't let me be.
The canvas of tomorrow waits for a splash,
While I juggle my thoughts like a juggling bash.

At times I wonder if I'm just a joke,
A clown on a stage, pushing thoughts to provoke.
But laughter's my paint, with confidence bright,
Creating a picture that feels just right.

So here's to tomorrow, a day full of fun,
With canvases waiting, and no need to run.
In the art of uncertainty, let's waltz beneath stars,
Creating a life full of glitter and bars!

Embracing the Gray Horizons

In the land of mixed signals, we stand,
Waving at choices like they're a band.
With a map that's a doodle, and snacks in hand,
We plunge into gray, isn't it grand?

A decision at breakfast, toast or jam,
A choice so weighty, I feel like a ham.
Life's twists and turns are one big exam,
But who needs a plan? Just get up and scram!

With coffee in hand, we chase after dreams,
Bouncing through wonders and whimsical schemes.
I laugh at the chaos, it's just as it seems,
In a world full of riddles, absurdity beams.

So let's celebrate chaos, embrace the delight,
In the fog of confusion, we'll dance through the night.
We're all just lost travelers, and that feels right,
With humor our compass, we'll be just alright.

Fragments of a Pathless Existence

In the museum of choices, where paths disappear,
I trip on my thoughts like I'm chasing a deer.
With fragments of wisdom, and snacks oh so near,
I ponder my life while sipping a beer.

Should I chase after sunsets or nap till I fade?
With options like confetti, we're all quite afraid.
Yet laughter's a sword that will never degrade,
So here's to the messes, let's dance in the shade!

Like puzzles with pieces that clearly don't fit,
I create my own rules, a life full of wit.
In the gallery of wonder, I freely admit,
The best art is chaos, let's make a big hit!

So I'll stroll through uncertainty with flair and a grin,
Making peace with the mayhem, it's all a win-win.
Life's just a jigsaw, with laughter to spin,
In fragments of nothing, let the journey begin.

The Dance of Question Marks

In a ballroom of whims, we twirl all around,
With question marks leading, there's magic profound.
Each step a conundrum, with giggles abound,
We cha-cha through doubts, on unsteady ground.

Should we tango with yes, or simply decline?
The rhythm of life is a waltz by design.
With each twist and turn, we blend fate and wine,
In this dance of confusion, we're feeling just fine.

So let's pirouette through the fog and the haze,
With chuckles and grins, we'll mosaic the maze.
In the ballet of chaos, let's make our own praise,
For life's just a stage where uncertainty plays!

With shimmies and shakes, we embrace the unknown,
In a cast of question marks, we've happily grown.
Let's groove through the puzzles, together we've flown,
In this dance through existence, we're never alone.

Finding Solace in the Uncertain

In gardens of chaos, we plant silly seeds,
With laughter as sunlight, and whimsy as weeds.
We nurture our doubts, and see what it breeds,
In the pot of uncertainty, we find our creeds.

Should I bake with the lemons or throw them away?
With a dash of absurdity, I'm here to stay.
Each question a recipe, twirling in play,
In the kitchen of living, let's sauté our gray.

As clouds drift in sky-fights, I raise an eyebrow,
With humor my shield, I weave through the wow.
In the tapestry of life, I'll figure it out,
With threads of confusion, let's triumphantly plow!

So here's to the moments that wiggle and sway,
The jests and the jigs that pepper our day.
In the solace of nonsense, we'll frolic and play,
For finding the funny will always lead the way.